Sleeping in Tall Grass

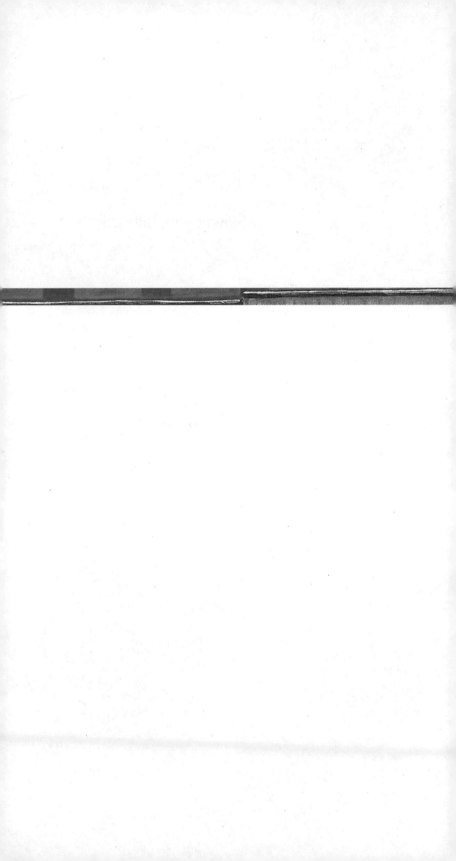

Sleeping in Tall Grass

Richard Therrien

 THE UNIVERSITY OF ALBERTA PRESS

Published by

The University of Alberta Press
Ring House 2
Edmonton, Alberta, Canada T6G 2E1
www.uap.ualberta.ca

LIBRARY AND ARCHIVES CANADA CATALOGUING IN PUBLICATION

Therrien, Richard, author
    Sleeping in tall grass / Richard Therrien.

(Robert Kroetsch series)
Poems.
Issued in print and electronic formats.
ISBN 978-1-77212-122-3 (paperback).—
ISBN 978-1-77212-155-1 (pdf)

    I. Title. II. Series: Robert Kroetsch series

PS8639.H4745S54 2016   C811'.6   C2015-908763-5
                                           C2015-908764-3

First edition, first printing, 2016.
Printed and bound in Canada by
Houghton Boston Printers, Saskatoon,
Sakatchewan.
Copyediting and proofreading by
Alice Major.

A volume in the Robert Kroetsch Series.

The University of Alberta Press is
committed to protecting our natural
environment. As part of our efforts,
this book is printed on Enviro Paper: it
contains 100% post-consumer recycled
fibres and is acid- and chlorine-free.

The University of Alberta Press
gratefully acknowledges the support
received for its publishing program
from the Government of Canada, the
Canada Council for the Arts, and the
Government of Alberta through the
Alberta Media Fund.

Government of Canada | Gouvernement du Canada   Canada Council for the Arts | Conseil des Arts du Canada   Alberta Government

In memory of my brother Claude
1950–2015

Who am I, and who
Lives in the carnival behind my eye?
　　　—Gwendolyn MacEwen, *The Carnival*

If then you perceive me, you perceive yourself.
But you cannot perceive me through yourself.
It is through my eyes that you see me and see yourself,
Through your eyes you cannot see me.
　　　—Muhyiddin Ibn al-'Arabi, *The Book of Theophanies*

The light and the eyes it invents to detain it are two
silences, one radiance, many
unfinished yet fully
complete conversations.
　　　—Robert Bringhurst, based on Xiangyan Zhixian
　　　　(9th cent.)

CONTENTS

I

Walking the prairie is telling the poem
its cadence rising matter-of-factly from the swell and fall
of her great grass belly   sharp prairie light peeling syllable
from syllable   —telling the poem
is stopping the sun
the narrative
in telling   never told
                —history
without a foothold
the plains   are taking hold
              —*It is not*
          my teachers say
              the will that dissolves the ego.
They said:
      Your heart is but a quiet place for the poor
      wandering universe to rest its weary head.

Walking the prairie is sailing inward   daughter
mother of the sea   generation
is reciprocal   horizon
refusal:
              You may walk forever into my embrace
              but this tender enfolding of gaze into image   these
              fields of light will never be breached

You bury your father
        and later will come to visit
        and the earth that holds him will speak softly
        then listen with rapt attention for your reply

My daughter on the edge of the circle of mourners
her tiny hands twisting the trim of her pale blue dress.

There is this Death, this ugliness and there is
this other thing, light as a dream, this
weakness without shame. These large men moving about
awkward in their clean stiff bodies borrowed for the afternoon.

I shall never again, this is how I read her sealed lips
and hard stare. *Never again will I be this afraid, there is nothing, now,
to be afraid of.*

SALT

There is a light that expires in my mouth.
—Georg Trakl

Once there was —the moment
blasted blinded

Where the tangent looking back
touches the curve of time we turn

to salt I re⁄call

the glance Lot's wife turning
in her pastel robes in the pastel desert
watching the pastel city burn —*Bible Stories for Children*
open on my lap —Lot's children huddled
in the corner of my room listening to the sound
of their mother's bones
turning to salt

Hidden in the glory of the sun   the promise
of dark loam the embracing reluctance
of decay   the aroma that draws flesh to soil

Kneeling on southern slope
ear to the bending heliotrope
I hear the names of the Paraclete
and embrace their passing

Granite Erratic
Slough
Gilead bud
Sik'sika
Red-tail
Coulee

My emptiness will not be
frenetic with the friction
of my father's silences

but still as the unmarked graves
of his many forgotten selves

The rain's soft as gold now   expect it any time
the hour in the middle of the night when we all suddenly wake
without a word

the object of refuge
                    book
                    hammer
                    orchid

unfolds at the hand of will   sung   danced
played into view for the pleasure of light

Building the past   this future we step into may
or may not be co-incident with
Parousia   the advent coming at us full force   entering
the now whose door a rosebud opens by
free will alone   sunlight
and the magpie's brushing wing

humility   willful surrender   these the tools
for negotiating with time   for wiping clear
the lens of apperception   accuracy possible
only through the silence

of the nesting crane   the child
dancing in the meadow

> *lover beloved craftsman healer*
> *two-handed making   the rest is hubris envy and slavery*

II

WATER, LANGUAGE, FAITH

hope is such

snow deep brilliant sun

winter dogteeth biting cheeks the few
of us out nod one to the other along the river
downtown towers rise up mountains
out of the clouds the edge against the nuance
books in my knapsack   leaving the library
a man talking to his reflection in the window
the enormous tragedy of the dream
in the peasant's bent shoulders

crossing the Bow via Centre Street Bridge then
up along the escarpment now in stiffest wind nothing
but one foot in front of the other head down shoulders
up against the glare the cold a voice *but then but then after*
the end the end of thought the words to naught

Guy Davenport says the work of the poet is continuous
while other ways of telling are wildly discontinuous
they forget the past   stopping and starting
but the poet   says Davenport   works his melodies
into the very grain of existence

—or grain meaning staff of life   northern wheat planted
in the fall   winter rye what an amazing invention
dreaming of first thaw   waiting
for the generosity   of lengthening light

—or in the spring my father after Sunday mass in the yard
with his hoe spade axe   anything
to break up the ice   coax its melting
get the water running towards the alley
over April's still frozen lenten black mud
        —water   he would say   standing over
his chinook-warmed drainage-works
                    always finds its own level

dad on the phone says mom's getting weaker can't eat
it's the chemo that's killing her he says   I know that

she says she has no choice he says they don't
give you a choice   take the chemo
or you'll be dead in three months
that's what they told her
what kind of choice
is that

he says

hope I guess
he says

everyone wants to live

then another pause   then we talk politics
hockey

Or other times talking about an accident maybe
somebody killed or some other unsolvable puzzle
or his war years on the minesweeper drifting
through mine-littered waters waiting
to be blown unannounced   into oblivion
                    —why would some thrive on that
he would ask   being shit-scared like that   and not others
    he would muse   sitting on the hood of his '65 Plymouth
                        lifting his bottle in a toast to Orion
                    —going to bed at night meeting
your ship-mate's eyes   down below deck   hammocks swinging
from the rafters
                    —wondering Is he the one?   Who will it be
who in the morning will be found hung by the neck
with a rope tied by his own hand?

—or something at work happened
and *water* my father would say   drink in hand
always finds its own level   and at his elbow or from
around the corner or down the hallway I would wonder
peering into his adult world   what water   what level?

Visible from the dining room table of my parents' home
a clock on the dishwasher a clock on the microwave a clock
on the stove a clock on the coffee maker a clock
on the wall above the table a clock
on the tv over there in the living room
and everything white *I've got an appointment
with the radiologist*

What for?

Your guess is as good as mine

Why did you make the appointment?

I didn't   my doctor did

Which doctor?

The oncologist   the nice one

What for?

I didn't ask   He's the nice one   he's really nice
not like the other one

Why didn't you ask?

Your father doesn't like it when I ask questions   your father's
not bad when you're here   when you come to visit
but as soon as he's alone with me   boy
You wouldn't believe it

He can be so mean.

Tu pers ta langue tu pers ta foi   this the warning
from her mother   my mother   young mother
took with her boarding the train in '52 leaving the forks
of the Assiniboine and Red Rivers   kids in tow
to join her husband already working west and north.

Riding the train across the prairie sailing
from valley to valley the plain rising
and falling away to nothing   standing on the seat
gripping the window-sill as we took flight
the trestle tucked in tight invisible under the floating locomotive
—*on vole! on vole!*   —through deepening prairie sky
    blue   nothing but blue   my gaze
dropping then stopping on sudden   disappointing
deep valley   bottom.

Tu pers ta langue tu pers ta foi   the word *assimilation*
comes in retrospect   a hearkening back a receiving
into the fold of language   suggesting a bringing in
a welcome   —but inside that exile
the truer word *déraciner* is all there is
—in the rip the tear itself, there as a child this
the dwelling place
—who ever thought the ground you stand on
grow your food in bury your dead in
could so easily open up from under you
—leave you suspended above nothing like prairie sky
pawing the loose threads of mother tongue   the child
trying to remember
hanging there.

Tu pers ta langue tu pers ta foi   riding the bus
with my mother our only time alone—in a family of seven
an oasis amidst the chaos—I would look forward to doctors'
appointments and other cross-town excursions
she would tell me things
warn me about things
women with too much makeup
people who pretend to have no fear
forgetting the language of your ancestors
the evils of atheism and science
the communists who would be converted if we prayed
to the holy virgin mother.

Tell me mother why you cried in the night so

what crying she would say *what are you talking about?*

I remember   I might have said

what do you remember she would ask
with a voice signifying things one ought not
to remember

the crying all night long that's all
    nothing else   I would answer to myself looking
down at my feet dangling from the blue plastic bus seat
—that same intangible field between my mother and I
now filled with the progress of cancer.

Tell me mother

well she might say *You know it wasn't*
easy back then
                followed by a long silence or an abrupt change of topic

and I would try another approach   Do you
remember what day of the week we left St. Boniface
who brought us to the train station?   was the sun
shining that day?

≈

So many women his mother's age he notices now
wearing wigs the similar pallid mask
their bodies once ennobled in childbirth
now dumping grounds for medicine's
crowning glory   chemical remission
husbands once their keepers
now dawdling behind in their incontinence
the look of slaves resenting everything exhausted
from their century of opportunity their
fill of fear.

≈

Doing floors rubbing lemon-scented melancholy
into hard wood grain   remembering
the drive south from Edmonton
Mom's chemo suspended for a week
so she wouldn't be sick through Christmas

Dad in the front passenger seat   Mom and my niece
in the back seat   my gaze a constant jittery sweep
over cropless snow-powdered contours   miniscule swaths
of left-over wild coulee

                    in the rear-view mirror
her kerchief tight over bald head   bright yellows
oranges   a touch of cornflower blue
she was down to ninety-some pounds by then
my niece's head leaning on mom's sloped bony shoulder
far from snug   co-conspirators   their feigned sleep
a carefully prepared bouquet for the child's future memory
crossing the Battle River somewhere near Red Deer
where the weather always changes

III

SLEEPING IN TALL GRASS

Thou art the spirit that gave birth to me, and
Thou art the child to whom my spirit gave birth.
—Suhravardi

You came lying flat on your back near the forks of the Assiniboine
and Red rivers, on the Riel side, you came naked and naked began
assembling your armour—memory—fragments of blue
at first it was all you could see, shards and patches of blue

I left you early within weeks of your arrival
my departure effortless

Every cell of your newborn body thrilled
to the sensation of my pulling away
the gentle airy tug at your thorax

then your mother, our mother
her smell her milk-warm glow

then you were floating, travelling
in one easy arc set down on the grass in the shade
closer to the hedge   out of the blazing sun
your eyes cast upwards pulling you up into
a single blue   nothing but blue

and history split into two

You came marked for the journey west already
knowing how to read the North Saskatchewan's
great meander, your lungs already knowing
how to gauge winter's thirty-below distances.

You came enraptured you came grief-stricken

I made you an apprentice thief   I taught you
how to approach the body with stealth

You came to swear an oath   —I came to show you
how to break it   how to temper parts of speech
into elegant weaponry   how to arm yourself
with escape clauses   I showed you how quickly
marks on the page could send you back to nothing
resembling time   matter or reason

You came to renew your innocence after the exhaustion
of spent rage   you came with the mark of the dreamt
the not quite present

You came unafraid of seduction   eager to fall
into the arms of the goddess   any goddess whose body
would teach you that patterns worth tracing lie not
on parchment   altar   or tongue

You came as a boy sleeping in tall grass under wind, back
flat against the earth, waking at age four to wander back
into your afternoon nap, the squeak of your mother's
ironing board and a faint radio tune
coming softly down the hall.

ABOUT A MILE FROM THE LAKE

for Larry, keeper of the fire

I.

Speak to be true
  along the rivers of the interior   ride out the event
be unconcerned

Speak to be true down along the valley bottoms
  anyone might follow us here

Speak to the seep of light rising from underfoot
  up through buffalo grass   through wild rose bramble
through ice-encrusted snow

Attend to the event

Follow the arc of the axe-head down the length of dried birch
  hear the split opening up its own sigh of relief   the hatchet
  raised once again
              —to this attend fully   let form sing itself up
  out of each descending blow

Follow your gaze out through the kitchen window
let yourself be drawn by pale sunlight   out of the cabin
into the bush out back   let yourself go with the sudden
temperature drop   pay no heed   to its clear brittle warning

Be attentive to the event   be unafraid of death's casual
40-below presence   leaning against the outside wall
waiting patiently for you
to open the door

Be deliberate   make the breach   tempt the icy shackling
of your blood   risk the very cease of movement   the stilling
of all molecular activity   the slowing
of the human pulse   to nil

Approach with measured step the pale fresco
of aspen and white birch   their pencil-thin outlines
cracks in a wall of frost

Ease your way towards the pole-straight winter-stark
poplar trunks   their long narrow shadows laid over
the surface of the billowing knee-deep snow

Stand with the scattered pine and blue-grey spruce
steadfast sentinels watching over this most ordinary patch
of land whose draw is as covert and fetching as barren can be

Wait for the frantic do-or-die birdsong to return
wait for their melodies to unravel the blanket of silence
brought down by the opening and closing of the cold-twisted
cabin door   —noisy aluminum jangle of nerves
sent shivering through the frozen body of air

Bend at the knee   bow to the small clearing that borders
the neighbour's property   be humbled before
the one lone pine that holds the centre of the clearing
an axis for a spray of deer tracks in and out

Turn away.

Begin the daily trek.

Put one foot in front of the other.

Draw and release the breath slowly   evenly

Avoid regret or reverie—a waste of oxygen best kept
in reserve for kindling the inner spark   the small sure leap
of spirit against the temptation to let the body be brought
to ground by the patient grip of ice crystals   slowly sealing
the nostrils and eyelids shut.

2.

Ravens crack open the sky   mock his daily ritual
                    —Here he comes again
headed for the winter-deserted village   hunched and hooded
heavy-footed in his seven layers of clothing and fake
sealskin Sally-Ann mukluks   grounded
by the soaring raven's watchful eye
      —from that airborne locus
he sees himself encased in his own trudging gait
and daily this point of view climbs higher
while below he shrinks unmercifully
grows ever more absurd   a foreshortened stain
on a vast sheet of snow   a solitary walker
with a vague hope of meeting some stranger
on the road
                    —usually marked with deer coyote ermine rabbit
                    and a few truck-tire tracks   but never
                    with human prints   —except his own
                    doubling back after the village loop

And today he imagines returning to no tracks leading out
from the cabin   as though he'd never been there at all
or worse   was still inside

3.

Beyond the edge of the aspen stand   a flutter of wings
a streak of grey obscured by meshed grey branches
—he suspects Whiskeyjack—the trickster *Wisakedjak*
movement and sound as intangible and real as the ancestors
buried in unrecounted wintercounts taking temporary shelter
in the ice-encrusted tree-wells beneath the pine

The stillness of the frozen deciduous stick-forest holds
the solitary man in its grip   the aspen's mottled green-grey
bark calling to his hand   coaxing him to remove
the sheepskin mitt   the attraction strong enough to reduce
the distance between bark and palm   to zero
palm and fingers molded to the trunk   the pleasure
of skin to skin   reciprocal

4.

Approaching from the east you don't see the lake
    you see its dream of ice and wind   its nebulous shore under
    a weak February sun indistinguishable from
    the surrounding hills hunched white
    under the low glowing steel-grey cloud cover

No time passes and you've stepped onto the ice and kept
moving   pushed your body step by deliberate step
through the wind's layered chorus   to stand
without orientation inside the lake's hollow haunt
    the four cardinal points   pointless

At your feet the sound of small sibilant ice crystals skittering
over the surface of the snow-packed ice   and above that
a thick sonorous breeze rides the drifts in from the hills
    and above that   the sound of a swollen airstream
    solid with celestial authority   a sigh so deep
    it could only be coming from within

Upright out on the ice marked by no horizon
you have no reason to move   only to stand
to wait   to listen

wind shaping vowel‑sounds looking for consonants
to rein its madness in
    sounds that sharpen your hearing and tune it to
    the unfamiliar nuances of ground‑gripped speech
    utterances that come unbidden   names lifted
    from the maps and research papers
    scattered across the table back in the cabin
    names remembered from the recent edition
    of the local *Pipestone Carrier*   names buried
    amongst ads for boating and fishing supplies
    septic tank services   snow removal   bingo

names whose brief sojourn through your memory have left
barely a trace   thinner than parchment   thin enough
to be peeled away from your tongue by the wind
      to be carried back to
            Neyaskwayak The Northern Tree Line
            back to
            Kishpahtinaw
                The Rise Before the Hill
            back to *Nipishkopahk*
          The Willow Meadow on the Banks of *Notinikewin*
The River of Battle Wounds

And here you stand   solid   with no desire to move
                        —I could collapse here
—the voice surprises you   it speaks   you think   not for you
    but for your bones   your pulse   your breath
                        —I could drop here

I could fall to my knees   lie prone
I could curl up on the ice and give in
to the warm temptation of sleep
I could freeze to death   here
I could live forever
here

5.

Brief touch of late afternoon sun   the snow withdraws
into itself   leaving a thin skin hardening   adorns itself
with a sprinkle of greeting-card sparkle before
the slip of evening lays itself down
to receive descending night

6.

I remember the day   the excitement
the slow build-up   the long drive into the country
the unveiling
    —father and son standing on the side of a dirt road
staring into dense bush

Impenetrable   I remember thinking

In the underbrush a plastic pink DayGlo ribbon
tied to a short square peg

His reasons for buying this indistinguishable
piece of property   —raw   in the middle of nowhere
at least a mile from the lake
                —a mystery to me

> *We'll clear over there, plant some evergreens along*
> *the property line, you'll see, it'll be beautiful*
> *we'll put the cabin up there on the rise*
> *over by the birch.*

> *It's for you* he says
> and I turn a brute shoulder
> a refusal to join him in his nobility
>   a father's need for a son's approval
>   urgent and secret   lost to me

Our memories an unwritten pact between brothers
an unsung song   a song that would sing the old man's heart
a heart that knew not its own rapacious rage   a song sprung
from a tongue that knew not its own loquacious lament
a song to sing the fire-pit   the circle of stones   to sing
the woodpile under the faded blue tarp   the horseshoe pit
the old outhouse   the dilapidated tool shed   an unsung song
to sing the remnants of the old man's will   a song sung
to be true to the worship of bonfire roar   and family lore

And blessed be   the sacramental booze   the leaping flames
the faces in a circle all alit

And praise be   the liturgical turn to melodrama   the sweep
of maudlin tears   the tired rites of self-expiation
the fire dwindling down to a 3 a.m. glow

the hangover morning the picking up
the washing up the packing up the retelling
of the night's humorous events

and sullen the return to the city
and its vertiginous   respectability

—we have all chopped wood here   my brothers and I
laid the tinder and kindling   stacked the wood just so
we have all struck the match   we have all
been dreamt into the dream of the father
willing this place   into being

7.

The airtight's low muted roar
the fire's off-beat explosive crackle and popping syncopation
holding the dark room in limbo
    table covered in books and papers
    the frantic sound of a pencil scratching
    making a thing   a capture of words pushing against
    obscurity   answering the call to perfection

The fire's crackle reduced to sputtering sparks
the old man's voice *It's for you*
launches the son up out of his chair to stoke the fire
                        —jams the poker jams the poker—
   It's for you   his constant harangue
   the old man's faithful expression   a family joke in the end
   what it means to have lived a good life
   to have left something behind   a piece of property
   a cabin   his simple version of an afterlife
   honouring a blood lineage   an emblem
   a clenched dream

8.

Wait for the nightly visitation

Listen for the crazy coyote choir
carving sonic designs out of the night

Strain your listening through layers of darkness
tune your ears   try to ascertain their exact number
or the strategy behind their manoeuvres

From deep within woodheat comfort let yourself rise
   retrace the moonlit map of trails and ravines
   over the mile and a half to the Bonnie Glen Field
   —600 million barrels of oil deep under *Maskwacis*

and howl with the Bear Hills Cree   howl the song
of Louis Bull's three teen suicides
and *Neyaskweyahki* Ermineskin's four-year-old
shot dead in her bed

howl with the Montana and Samson bands
oil-rich and gang-infested   between the number 2 Highway
   the 621 and the southeast shore of the lake   follow
   the howling back to your own breath and heartbeat
   to that stranger self sitting alone in the dark   follow
   the hollow sound   up from solar plexus   past larynx
   and out through top of skull   into the archaic promise
   of direct ascendance
       the vertical column of golden light promising
to hold time still intersecting with the endless horizontal
going out   the relentless topography tugging at your thorax
pulling you forth
            —here is the crux of the event
the collapse behind your ribcage
sinking with it the day's memories
the morning fire the morning brew
the afternoon trek the evening meal
      the animal trails that surround and pass through
      this small acreage that holds the cabin you know
      that daily greets the hands that built it
      the stories that keep it
          —though you know not
the land it sits on   not really   at least no more than
you have tramped through   or looked up on a map
the geography shifting where once it was steady
long before your family's historical inroads
from Imperial France   three-and-a-half centuries ago
to end up here   in the crux of the event
neither a point in time   nor a coordinate on a plane
        the deed   after all   still not cleared

9.

Retreat complete   he waits to be picked up
to be driven to the airport
sits staring out the front window   past the deck
into the small forest first glimpsed
forty years ago from the road

the road that was nothing but a dirt track
cutting through this diminutive riparian plain
whose waters   when not frozen
still feed the lake about a mile southwest of here

I may never return to this place

—the unexpected utterance empties him momentarily
of everything that holds his body in place
 I may never again occupy
   after all these years
 the body of   my father's dream

     —and from the right a white-tailed deer
illuminated by the late afternoon slant of sun
eases its way out of the shallow ravine
      glistening black nostrils   enormous eyes
      conical ears alert and scanning
      voluptuous neck thick with white fur
      strategic strokes of beige and brown
      upright tail like a sail

headed for the front clearing   with delicate steps   concise
and deliberate she moves through belly-deep snow

—then another deer   and another   and another
and another   nine in all   nose to tail
each in sync   with the others

they wind their way from pine to pine towards
thicker bush at the far rim of the clearing
silent ciphers one by one   gradually stitching
their invisibility   back into the trees

IV

BURNING OAK

Pungent earth
magnetic to the blood
electrifies the dancer   ecstatic
to the bone

We are made of language and our bodies made of air
the mind a temple built upon
a sea of broken promises
our tongues
must endlessly repair

our voices charged to name the names
that spread the rumour
of our having passed
this way

the breath a hairline fracture in the silence of our sleep
the hearth and unfed fire awaiting our return
—covert preparation for
our inescapable
escape.

Archaic tribes   have sent their scribes
to infiltrate your pages

The word aflame in the darkened branches
of your dreaming oak   falters   fanned
by the jittery sweep of your inner gaze

shaping glyph   word   line   as carefully
as fearfully as you choose a child's name
calculating how to pluck it out of the air
without disturbing its natural flight

Unable to incubate the silence   the mind
manic with hunger hunting first cause
final effect   the treachery of speech illuminated
by the dwindling light   of reason's failing appetite

you busy your hands with carving out
some perfect model of grief   using no measure
no plumb   no light   trying to force the form
into the exact dimensions
of your slippery body of thought

Refusing the easy worship of objects   crouching instead
under the bridge on the banks of the Caesura
the bowman listens for the signal that will spring the arrow
split the wind   open a path   between the ventricles
of this vast beating heart

the utterance coming face to face   finally
with the unutterable   the sovereign thing itself
wrapped in a burning sun of no mercy
for those who dare and fail

And if not Harmony
then who is sounding the trail

who is collecting the water spilling out of the rock
whose sad dream will the torch singer be singing tonight
who will recall the deep rest and comfort
of wordless wilderness

whose hammer-struck lyric (under whose cover of prayer)
will be carving out this song to the Sphinx's final raid
on reason's damp lair?

Forensic scholars will have been spotted poking through
the still glowing embers of your spent tongue

this is how you will wake to questions   this is how
you will be rendered mute

called as a witness to chronicle your rant   decipher
your cant   I will pass under the archway early   arriving
even before the television crews have finished setting up

how grand your court appearance

but you will lean on debate   you will want to say
that it was like a journey   that you fell from a hole
in the sky and were greeted by large men with racks
of antlers on their heads   you will refuse to explain
their sudden disappearance

you will say that you slept outside with the dogs
relentlessly dissatisfied   and the jury will hear
that you were oblivious to the magnetic attraction
of your own deep breathing   the seductive savagery
of your sleeping body   ghosts of language spilling
out of your eyes like buttermilk   moonlit
sour   everflowing

under cross-examination you will   finally   falter
Dreams   you will want to say   *dreams*
are carried in the blood   but protecting yourself
you will wisely bite your tongue

and I will be forced to testify how I watched you bargain
with Hermes   that fine old pimp working
his spell through the night before stepping back
into the darkened doorway of his after-hours club

I will want to say what it's been like all these years
waiting here in the garden   watching you work
the evidence through the night   watching you
scribble your way towards the final clumsy unveiling
of your perfectly constructed anachronistic illuminations

and I will have to describe how your own vicious hounds
tore you limb from limb   and fed on the very tongue
that once called them to the hunt

and you will confess that you had to speak obliquely
of your obsessive questioning   your failure as a mystic
and how you were prepared to stand under the mountain
ash   between the path and the river   hunted now
turning to face the bowman   letting his eyes and yours
decide which way   the sacrifice   would go.

Herakleitos says nature loves to hide
and Davenport re-translates—
Becoming is a secret process

Knee-deep in river water the fisher-poet casts
his line and brings a waterfall of magnolias
into bloom

but the heart sees directly into nature
and is overwhelmed by the becoming there

A new sun for every day
Herakleitos says (and ibn 'Arabi says
every moment a new configuration)
—and the sun is one foot wide he says
—and the most beautiful order of the world
is still   he says   a random gathering of things
insignificant in themselves

Moses in the desert   bewildered
trying to apprehend the disembodied voice:
Take the staff and strike the stone

—bleeding lip   jaw clenched
to contain the songs   the wailing
of saints and martyrs   spine

straining against the curve of human event
the liquid gathering of our senses and their far-flung objects
their refusal to be known

—sudden water from the rock   the flooding
of this vast beating heart

When Gabriel told Mohammad men sleep
and when they die they waken
this was no mere admonition
this was practical instruction in how to see

The poet occupies the dreaming mind   his or another's
makes no difference   not to bring the dream back
for interrogation   not to humiliate it with interpretation
but to return with its way of looking

V

I CAN'T REMEMBER
THE WEEKEND EXACTLY

Cross carved in air or on body
the memory muscular cellular
the cardinal points—the forehead the navel
the sinister shoulder the righteous right
and long before the age of reason
the holy trinity seared into the boy's
memory dazzled and dazed by the gesture

In sleep the smell of defilement coming off
my brother's whimpering body—this was
long before I understood how bodies
were things that could so easily be ravaged
long before I learned that the contagion
of terror could seep from the soul
of one innocent into the soul of another

In sleep the mute clatter of prayer escaping
the body pinned to the floor in the chamber
of heavenly authority—in sleep the sibilance
of whispering informants sliding across
the frozen prairie between the Northern
Saskatchewan junior seminary and home
—every wind-driven sliver of snow turning
every eye blind   every blind eye turning
away from every son's accusing eye
—how easily the horror of detail
can seal the lips and turn the heart
in a heartbeat hard with self-preservation

Somewhere on the Carlton Trail, Saskatchewan, 1963

High above the gas station closed for the night
a derelict Esso sign jangles in November wind.
A shivering boy on the run boxed in a phone booth,
blue glow pooling on dirty snow, older than a child
but a child still, crossing the frontier into the age
of reason, a territory where, other than the evil
in your own heart there can be no reason to sin.

A phone-shaped lump of frozen black plastic held
to his mouth, unable to find the words, the words
he cannot find, try as he might, will only be found
in years to come, the trembling shoulders a betrayal
the transgression fully his own—no confessor no mentor
can be to blame, the tongue tied in a tangle of guilt
and terror, the other father at the other end of the line
berating his son for making the call—*collect*—
when a bloody stamp only costs four cents
—you get back there *now*.

I knew the Lamb of God before I knew the lamb
the resurrected Christ before I knew the book
that carried him to slaughter, I knew my father
before I knew the Heavenly Father—the slow
stealthy absorption of one holy terror by another—
invisible and everywhere inescapable.

I knew the pastel Holy Mount rising off
the gilt-edged *Bible Stories for Children*
long before I knew actual mountains
—the Rockies approached from the East
rising off the horizon—the blue '58 Plymouth
station wagon lifting off the asphalt held
aloft by the awe of its passengers
the happy family on summer vacation

—and upon return—the mountain miracle carried
home in our bones, in our wonder, we anointed
ourselves into our new earth mystery—dug out
our own cave, a hole in the backyard between
the driveway and the vegetable garden, to lay
ourselves in, pulling an old stained and splintered
sheet of plywood over our curled-up bodies—there
to remain hidden in the dark, enjoying the cool protective
sepulchre of our own death and resurrection.

Ward 4A2, U of A Hospital, Edmonton Alberta, 2013

A hand—my hand—bringing a plastic spoon
of food to the droop of my brother's mouth
—he tries to chew—the mush like pale
tobacco chaw pouching up behind the useless lip

wiping his chin, helping him urinate
massaging his inert foot, delicate for a man

watching the good eye weep

shaving his lapsed face, the scruff resistant to
the old blade, both of us half expecting
dreading a sudden seep of blood

lying on his apartment floor, three days
trying to get up falling trying to get up falling
—trying to get his half-paralyzed body
to obey the commands of his struck mind
—thump thump thump over the head
of his downstairs neighbour who finally
decides to check it out

three bloody days—repeated often
from the hospital bed—and every time
at this point in the narrative a chill descends
—the listener's sliding look away—three days
no one calling—we become the body on the floor

and *no* we do not say
I will not we dare not say
this will not be the manner
of my *dying.*

I watch him sleep, a boy and I a big brother.

He stirs, he wakes, I smile, he falls back to sleep then wakes.

Always the hallway bustle the low-frequency hum
the machines, visitor, staff and patient conversations,
fuzzy ghosts of gossip bobbing on the surface of this
antiseptic always shifting pool of drug-muted suffering
—snowstorms and small-town politics, hockey scores,
neighbourhood misdemeanours and family intrigue
job promotions and bail hearings.

Between his waking and falling back to sleep,
in the rising and sinking we go in tenderness
to where no words are needed, the silence
thick with the presence of our father who died
seventeen years ago in this very ward, one stroke too many.

The beast that possessed our father till his dying day
now by my brother's own stroke brought to ground
laid at our feet like an invisible carcass opened up
with precise surgical caution, one glance at a time between
brothers, one buried accusation, one remembered
judgement at a time, memories long running underground
remaining fluid seeping to the surface now, carefully
fracturing the silence, troublesome territory once
circled and avoided now bids us enter.

You know they tried to give me money. I went to see
the parish priest at Mary Immaculate someone
recommended him. I told him my story. Sent me to
someone else, a specialist, they have specialists
for this kind of thing, this was four or five years ago.
A priest. Nice guy, good listener, really sympathetic
asked me what I wanted to do but I didn't know.

I just had to talk to someone. He asked me
if I wanted money I said no.

I thought he was kidding at first. But no there's money
available. Not to shut me up I don't think.

They recognize the cost, how it fucks you up all that
the alcoholism can't keep a job can't stay married
all that stuff.

Turned me right off, the money thing. Right off.
But to be honest I did think about it later. For maybe
a minute. You know, you think, I mean I could do
a lot of good with that money, help out my kids for once.

Then suddenly it hit me. I could see the bastard
right there like he was in front of me—handing me
a wad of bills I could see his face, his pudgy hand
pushing the money at me trying to pay me off, I mean
what would that make me? I felt sick to my stomach
I wanted to kill the bastard, it was the first time
after all these years that I wanted to hurt him, physically,
really hurt him. I never felt that before. It really shook me.

Still feeling fresh from his morning bath
crisp and bright in his plain white shirt
a little hungry from the pre-Eucharistic fast
the boy lifts his head slowly, soaks up
the warm deep glow saturating the inside
of his closed eyelids then opens his eyes,
then his mouth, to the light thin wafer
cool on his tongue. And he feels, without doubt
at the pious age of six the body of the crucified one
melting in his saliva, sliding down his throat
dissolving in his blood.

And the pederast who gives also takes away
—this is how it works, this he has figured out
puzzling out the mystery in the dark, forehead
pressed against his knees held tight to his chest
the back of his head pressed against the underside
of the basement stairs. It is from this damp grotto
that the penitent will be set loose to rove and sniff
the air, to carry in his gut a two-edged hunger
a steel trap of perpetual predation, perpetual escape
learning the signs, the right words to say
the misdirection and feigning patter, learning
to say earth while meaning blood, learning
to say utter devotion while meaning exhaustion,
learning to say hope while meaning the dream
running nightly over charred roots and blackened
stones, learning to stay one step always ahead of belief.

I can't remember the weekend exactly
I remember he just showed up
he wasn't supposed to be home
I remember a lot of whispered
shouting behind closed doors a lot
of seething silence—he never said anything
to me and probably not much more to them
we played ping-pong in the basement
—I remember that and he remembers that too
and Sunday after mass he was on the bus
and for the first time I could remember
I wondered if I'd ever see him again
though I had no idea why
—I didn't want to know
my mother's red eyes were enough
my father's stony look carved
with a sharper edge than usual
shame mixed with anger cutting deeper
more forbidding than knowing could ever be

A dozen or so stroke patients in a circle of wheelchairs
doing their physio—young, skinny, grizzled, polished, proud,
sullen, middle-aged, elders, Caucasian, Asian, Native
all wearing the same thin blousy pastel-coloured gowns
—making gargantuan effort to raise a floppy hand
a crooked foot, to keep the head up—sheer will
to keep the pink balloon afloat
the physiotherapists cheering them on
flashes of joy or resentment, the balloon
falls and is kicked, punched, struck with a limp hand
poked with an elbow, bounced off a shaved scalp split
down the middle with a wide stapled incision, a cartoon zipper

the balloon rising and falling, the unpredictable airy dance
of the pink balloon—and in those craniums new neurons
replicating new bloodways tunnelling into grey matter
comatose muscles beginning to remember—this
is the necessary infusion of hope, the payoff
for these tireless heroic athletes.

No no, no I never I never contacted him
thought about it years later
when I was in rehab
but no I couldn't
he's dead now I heard
I heard they shipped him out to South America somewhere
to work with the poor
just like they say
they say they just move them around that's what they do
maybe someone else another one of his victims or somebody
maybe blew the whistle
they say he was known for his work with children
there in Brazil
or whatever
renowned they say for his work with children
the poor the downtrodden all that
that's what they say they say the children loved him
even got an Order of Canada before he died
imagine
that's what I heard
for his work with children

My brother is about to stand.
On one good leg.
For the first time since his stroke.
Facing a full-length mirror. Two physiotherapists
have him in hand, one stands behind,
the other harnessed to his weak side
with a thick strap, the wheelchair
locked in front of the mirror, his right hand
gripped around a shiny steel pole, knuckles white,
he wants to get this right, his left arm hanging
uselessly in a sling. Then:
One... Two, *and... Up!*

Fear, inelegance—and will.

Somehow he is vertical. My brother had been
so absorbed in the gargantuan task, focusing
so hard on his own torso and limbs
that he hadn't looked up until reaching
this full standing position. Now,
he spots himself in the glass
and is shocked to see this gaunt ghost
in a flimsy hospital gown, this pale post-stroke
apparition he fails for several seconds
to recognize as himself

It sets him trembling
it's okay it's okay his attendants whisper
it's okay

But he is caught aghast in the mirror, tears
welling up in him and in me too standing off
to the side, surprised by his surprise
at this mercilessly brittle illustration
of his body's sudden demise

I am watching his gaze, the slow deliberate
drinking in of himself

Observing these few moments of private heroism
sends me back to the North Saskatchewan,
the south bank—well into adulthood but boys
nonetheless, we are skipping stones along the surface
of the water and ambling along, perusing
riverside gravel for the perfect shape, I am several
feet behind him and I watch him reach down,
I see his fingers pick up one stone among many
leaning on another, surprisingly smooth,
at its core the cool memory of fire
a longing to return to a place
impossible to name.

He doesn't pitch the stone but holds it tight in his fist
and continues walking along the shore, his bones,
his spine, his legs liquid. I watch him ride the rise
and fall of the aquifer deep beneath our feet,
I watch him walk with that smooth cautious lope
of the deeply injured some mistake for swagger.

Night has fallen. We build a small fire
the flames painting the wall of night flat black
to keep out the thing that wants most to be spoken
—always there especially when it's only him and me
and the night and a bottle, sitting still with heads bowed
or faces up braving the fire's heat, the shale at our feet
polished by the moon to a grey milky sheen. Suddenly
a rustle of bush to his left—a jump in his heart
a quasar from eons ago remembering the meaning
of alone sitting in the fire without a home.

They go in through the thigh just above the knee. Into the vein with a catheter, work it up the leg all the way to the carotid artery, imagine. Then release a tiny umbrella to catch any plaque that might break off and do more damage.

Then a balloon to expand the narrow blocked passage. Install the stent.

The whole operation takes an hour and a half. I watched the whole thing on the screen, the doctor talked me through it, I could actually feel them going in, I could feel the blood rush into my brain when it broke through. Imagine. After being starved for oxygen all that time.

My heart stopped for seven seconds, shut right down, that's what they said, I don't remember that part. The doctor said I scared the hell out of the nurses, my body started thrashing around then I came back, seven whole seconds, imagine. No tunnel of light or any of that.

The doctor working his little joystick, did the whole thing with a joystick, I watched it on the big screen but it wasn't like it was me up there, no, not at all.

In the centre of an empty room an upright
body facing a large upright mirror,
the floorboards of the shiny walnut-
stained floor clearly drawn to converge
on a distant point swallowed too soon
by darkness, I am the upright body
looking into the mirror and I see my brother
I hear my brother asking Who are you?
every syllable and consonant pronounced
with the precise tensile strength and sure
pressure needed of a larynx and vocal folds
ordered to contain, restrain, release
what can never be said what must be said,
I look in the mirror I see my brother I hear him
speak, my lips as static as the brilliant red wax
lips we used to buy from the corner candy store,
we are not twins my brother and I, not twins,
he was born ill two years after me and I
was born ill with him, he was defiled
years later and I, across the prairie under
a different sky and three watersheds east
was defiled with him, this is not a confusion
of confessions, this is not some Catholic
penitent trying to sing the sonorous call
of another's pain back to its subterranean birth,
not a stone struck ringing up from the bottom
of a dry dark canyon, this is blood, not
the blood of brothers, thicker than that,
this is blood symbolized by blood, voice
symbolized by voice, this is air, air
being shoved this way and that by two hearts
beating, one in an empty room, the other
in a mirror.

VI

LIVING ON AIR

Yeshua subverting the dogma of the elders
quoting the prophets radicalizing his tribesmen
freeing himself from the bindings of his beliefs
—is this not what every father desires for his son?

Eloi Eloi Lama Sabachthani

deserted because that is what gods   do

From the finely tuned precariousness
of physical survival and the cunning
of environmental adaptation—avian power

The sudden lift a moment of cedar grace

green fan sprung, needles soft as plumage

Synthesis and grace dance chlorophyll to light
Mountain and crocus sing falcon to flight

As bark is bound to wood and wood
to tree's core   we are bound   to surrender

Brought to light under the Chinook Arch
walking   one foot   galaxies later   in front of the other
striding through coulee vale and slough   defying wind
wind swinging open and shut you can send yourself
through that gate in or out makes no difference   leave
yourself behind   departure of the sweetest kind
silence singing your praises   will not reward you
nor relinquish   a pinch of your pain

there is no reason for this gift of seeing
turned to music then to mist

Dusk, and under the window on the table
the unlit candle translucent with fading light
—the wick calling memory's hand to strike the match
    come   bring me
    to completion

Inconceivable to attribute free will to myself
and not to the candle burning

Until the candle is burning it is not completed
and not completed   not a candle

This we share living on air

Perpetual movement seeking an object   a name
a river perhaps   becoming verb

River:
the most beautiful name of cause and effect
moving to the firm hand
of the loving   lay of the land

Coyote's yellow-toothed breath   wakes you

wanting love from the woman
who sleeps in the back of your throat

an open casket somewhere
a warm breeze leaves a chill
you hadn't expected

falling, falling back to sleep you seek
the scourge of angels who would benefit
from such generosity of madness

Dawn   begs earth
to stay

Through vowel
spirit enters
in consonant the soul

river's primal speakers
bind breath to flesh to bone

Grey brittle stars
the small cloven hooves
of morning

Between the lifting
of the eyelid
          and the glance
a speck of dust
          descending
arising

Meister Eckhart says
The creator has no within.

What needs doing gets done somehow
dance doing it beautifully

The plant oracle says
Nature responds with no arrangement of forced effort

There is the thing named
says Doctor Maximus *which is not
the same as the name and neither is the splendour aroused
by the naming the same as the naming itself*

When then after the language broken   opens   and night
swallows the remnants of ocean flowing down her spine
   loving will be told in intricate detail and fine ceremonial
embroidery   hope will be said in the looking back
   the face   naked finally   to the face
the tragic promise of self-transcendence lost
· in the word   incompletely   apprehended

Night
No sign of game

Stars
unfettered in their movement
magnetize the dance
slow it to
perfection

Wind forces the pause
the turn inward

Voices travel the night
soft, heavy with fertility   Night
binds father, shadow
back to back
draws mother, moon
breast to breast
the hunter's unsung secrets
burning out at sea

Hands
weightless with desire
praising the moon

not hunting   too   is hunting

every night a winter a story
left with voice
to trace the body
of this breath

In sleep the negotiating takes place
the terms of approach
the dance of elegant construction stripped
to brief hard light

every morning a birth
cold   chasing movement   in winter
we cannot stay still
for long

Where the Livingstone Range outruns its thrust
its riverrun wealth lays itself down spreads itself out
under the big broken reach of its straggling
cottonwood army   empties itself into the Bow
          the view east from Hailstone Butte   biblical

a favourite perch from which to witness the river's
prodigal run south then east then north and seaward
to the Hudson's Bay

and fire opening up the plains   sage bouquet   the scent
               a signal to meadowlark sent
against lament

               —Red-tailed Hawk
        rising on heat
               unshackles sight   from seeing

I hear a voice I remember three things

Time is a condition of landscape.

Nature responds with no arrangement or forced effort.

Look.

HEAVENLY MEN

part way through a murder mystery the roar
of the stadium crowd a half-mile outside his bedroom
window awakens the skin of his right arm turns it into
liquid sapphire, the sensation, the vision

paralyzed he can't put the book down, ciphers
on the page taking the shapes of their named,
lifting off the paper, scattering

but you must have slept
there must have been comfort under the quilt
describe to me the luxury of sleep

the instruments have been put away, the drapes drawn
the labourer sleeps peacefully
a pair of black swans at the river's edge
prepares for a long autumn flight, the executioners
disturb their wives with restless sleep. There is no luxury.

We doze, our limbs entangled,
our hearts tender as the darkening hills

what is the exchange here, where is daily bread?

we keep most of our clothes in cardboard boxes
on the floor of the bedroom closet we have
no vanity no chest of drawers
outside the night-window a dark-suited woman walking
through an equinox of incandescent light—2 seconds

at the most curtain to curtain—her sad smile
her looking away gathered up by eyeless street-wanderers
—heat-seeking hearts craving milk warm milk—
and across the street behind living-room curtains
the silhouette of a man sitting on his couch looking into
the palms of his hands searching the lines and calluses
for a way out of blame

I know many such men this is where we live

name the bonds that offer you protection

—river drinking the setting sun
—one pebble's shadow falling on the next
—the slow imperceptible cooling of stone

and where is the impulse to conviviality?

—lovers crossing the mist to enter the presence of oak
—the ravaged huddled in pain holding their bodies upright

by which nation does your family make its vows?

we carry no identification and greet the downtown worker
always, with equanimity

from time to time we find ourselves estranged
speech half a century behind our memories
so we send ourselves to stand side by side overlooking
the river—any river will do—there to negotiate
weather patterns in the realm of death and dying
—the how-to and the preparation-for

then we drink and laugh and gaze into our words and phrases
as though they stood as places where we might one day come to rest
and we talk our way around those objects we assume

we will one day have the heart to turn our backs on—such as
the arc we call horizon between the near and the forgotten

describe the dangers on which you build your sacred sites

—an unexpectedly smooth surface
—a climber taking to the air
—blood rising through moss

what colour is the soil in the fist of the grieving widow?

mother's milk mixed with dust from
stones hewn to mark our gate

from which common ground does the flora
of your language grow?

the veil of heat in a crowded cafe
breath leaping from mouth to mouth—a hand
closing around the warm mug
light escaping her body through the marks
on the back of her hand   around her eyes   her neck
her fingers unfolding from around the mug then rising
to the back of her neck to knead the tension there

and she turns towards the window?

                    —and we turn with her turn
the turn puts us outside on the sun-filled plaza with
the object of her gaze   a dalmatian on a short leash
the black leather strain of restraint the bulging eyes
the quivering flanks the urgent canine need to play
                    —and she turns back
lowers her eyes   light re-entering her body
as quickly as it had left

and heat what about heat?

a thirst like no other—glaze, baked mud, the kiln stoked,
daemons summoned, orange, red, the blue
of yellow sulphur's flame   wind's tattoo fixed by fire to the
vessel

then the cup is cooled?
                              —and raised

where do you place your tongue?

gently at rest in the bottom of my mouth barely touching
the curve of my teeth, the back of it raised slightly then
lowered to let the liquid slip through

describe the wilderness that lulls your elders to sleep
keeps your little ones awake

the wild expanse of concrete between the roadway
and the museum   the tamed secret that still corrodes
the parchment of our treaties
the worried faces turning away in the marketplace
the old man in the shadow of Bow Valley Square on Sixth
Avenue bending to pick up a discarded bus ticket
—it reminds him of the quinella he lost at the track
half a continent away—in the one blue eye gone lazy you see
not his thoughts but the quality of his thoughts, you know
these thoughts though not their names—the bus ticket
is a winning quinella stub inadvertently thrown away
at the track of his youth—and in the time it takes him
to bend and close his fingers around its upturned corner
you see the possibilities of fortune revealed
in his gentle movement   and your eyes
are refreshed by the charmed gesture

This city is filled with such heavenly men

Later in his room—up two flights of piss⁄reeking stairs
—a sink, a bed, a table—wolves will come out
from behind the calendar—*Stan's Autobody*—and above
the days of the week numbered through December
the glossy picture finger⁄smudged—on the edge
of a small emerald lake under a canopy of cedars
the impossibly pale voluptuously virgin madonna
is lifting her sky⁄blue skirt dipping her foot
into the mist⁄shrouded water
—the old man's hand turns the knob of his
small pale yellow plastic radio on the counter next
to the sink below the calendar   the frequency
set by his wife dearly departed seventeen years ago
—then slowly raising his hand his fingers gently closing
around the air that holds the perfection of his gift—a toast
    to the blue⁄skirted madonna, barely a whisper:
                    december december
                            forever december
—his empty hand to his lips.

by which marks do you tally the casualties of your hunger?

scars   marks of age   of loving worry
marks that trace the lines of want
marks on paper marks on wood   pressed to clay
marks to worship faces by
marks to draw a hungry eye

and from whose hand is this melancholia distributed?

the one whose strong fingers have been set against
the rigor mortis of my jaw to place this coin under my tongue
the one who will take me across the river to the old crone
eating alone in the garden

and what will be your angle of departure?

the small triangular shard of glass leaning against
the curb after a spectacular car crash

and what will mark your resting place?

an empty bowl in a pool of light on a wooden table
in an abandoned farmhouse   dust on its rim
waiting for the soft touch of breath

ENVOY

A hand gently striking the jawharp's tongue
tempered steel drawn into strange song
a voice singing of its own forgetting
heavy work-boots shuffling a soft jig
on a hard dirt floor.

NOTES

I

Sik'sika

The *Sik'sika* (Blackfoot, *the people*) live in what is now Southern Alberta—
the land of *N'api*, Old Man. The headwaters of the Oldman River in the
Livingstone Range, now dammed, is the place from which the world was
created.

Parousia

"Parousia" is a tricky word. Traditionally, in exegeses of the Synoptic
Gospels, the word is translated as *coming*, and projected further into *the
second coming*. In ancient Greek it breaks down literally as *alongside* and
carries connotations of *arriving*, *advent*, *appearing*, and primarily *presence*.

All derivations seem to stretch between motion and rest, which brings
me precisely to the sense in which I use it in this poem. In a Gnostic
fragment from the Gospel of Thomas, Yeshua instructs his disciples to
respond to questions regarding where they come from with the answer
from the place where light came into being by itself; that they are *children of the
light*; and if pressed, that they should say the evidence of their lineage lies
in *motion and rest*. Any arrival, appearance or advent, any coming—or any
second coming for all that—is, in other words, always and eternally present.

This accords with an earlier fragment from Thomas in which Yeshua
says: *Know what is in front of your face and what is hidden from you will be
disclosed to you.* The Gnostic view is also a direct challenge to the Ptolemaic
texts that equate *parousia* with the arrival of a king or emperor in some
distant future, and counters the primitive Advent text (from which Pauline
hope, alas, springs eternal): "Behold, thy king cometh unto thee." The
Gnostic Yeshua seems to be saying: No. Thy king is here. Now. In
plain sight.

II

the enormous tragedy of the dream
in the peasant's bent shoulders

Ezra Pound, from Canto LXXIV.
Pound's original is presented as a single line.

Guy Davenport

Davenport has been referred to as one of the last pure modernists. The author of over two dozen books, including poems, short stories, translations of ancient Greek texts and literary criticism, he died in 2005.

Tu pers ta langue tu pers ta foi

You lose your (mother) tongue, you lose your faith.

III

Thou art the spirit that gave birth to me, and
Thou art the child to whom my spirit gave birth

This quotation is Henry Corbin's take on Suhravardi's take on "Perfect Nature," or the celestial twin, from the *Corpus Hermeticum*. Suhravardi was a Kurdish Sufi mystic (b. 1154). Corbin was one of the first Europeans to study the Sufi tradition. See Henry Corbin's *The Man of Light in Iranian Sufism* (Shambhala Publications, 1978). See also *The Way of Hermes, New Translations of the Corpus Hermeticum* (tr. C. Salaman, D. Van Oyen, W.D. Wharton, Inner Traditions, 2000).

Wisakedjak

Some (mostly Algonquin) say *Wisakedjak*, others (mostly Cree) say *Wîhsakecâhkw*. We (mostly European settlers) say Whiskeyjack. Technically, it refers to the Grey Jay. In whatever language it also means *trickster*—with good reason; anyone who has camped in the Rockies, foothills, and parklands of Alberta and British Columbia will be familiar with their cheeky picnic-marauding ways and ingenious tricks for separating hiker from trail mix.

If I were to have a totem for my winter retreats at the cabin, it would be the Whiskeyjack. It is the only songbird that nests and lays its eggs in the dead of winter, usually February, in territories that are often plunged well into double-digit below zero temperatures. The birds line their nests with moss and fur foraged from carrion and roadkill, and feed themselves with lichen digested and regurgitated into sticky gobs that they press to the underside of tree branches and distribute throughout their territory for later harvesting. They are highly socialized; offspring remain part of their family unit for several generations, taking turns sitting on the eggs, foraging, lining the nests to keep warm, and feeding their younger siblings.

Maskwacis

Maskwacis (Bear Hills) is the original Cree name, now revived, for the settlement once called Hobbema. The settler name was given in honour of Dutch landscape painter Meindert Hobbema, who happened to be the favourite painter of Sir William Cornelius Van Horne, president of the Canadian Pacific Railway. Many Albertans are all too familiar with the tragedies of the Hobbema Indian Reserve that have perennially haunted the news. (My own parents would threaten to drop us off at the reserve on the way to the lake property if we didn't behave—*quelle horreur!*) The replacement of the settler names with Indigenous names is a good piece of medicine, not insignificant to the healing that needs to take place between the settler nation and the First Nations.

The vast difference—to the ear and to the open heart—between the uttered names *Hobbema* and *Maskwacis*—rings clear and true. For the profound philosophical implications of losing and reviving First Nations languages see Umeek E. Richard Atleo's *Tsawalk: a Nuu-chah-nulth Worldview* (UBC Press, 2004). For (often hilarious) insights into the advantages of multilingualism see Tomson Highway's *A Tale of Monstrous Extravagance: Imagining Multilingualism* (University of Alberta Press, 2015).

Herakleitos

This Presocratic philosopher is most famous for giving us "The river in which you stand is not the same river into which you stepped." Peter Kingsley has spent decades brilliantly demonstrating that the so-called Presocratics—in particular Parmenides and Empedocles—were in fact Greek shamans, and the spiritual founders of Western civilization. See *In the Dark Places of Wisdom* (The Golden Sufi Center, 1999), and *Reality* (The Golden Sufi Center, 2004).

VI

Eloi Eloi Lama Sabachthani

Father, Father why hast Thou deserted me...

The plant oracle

...is a traditional moniker for the *I-Ching*.

Doctor Maximus

Muhyiddin Ibn al-'Arabi, a 13th-century Sufi mystic, was born in 1165 in Andalusia and died in 1240 in Damascus. See *Creative Imagination in the Sufism of Ibn 'Arabi* (Henry Corbin, Bollingen Series XCI, Princeton University Press, 1969).

When Gabriel told Mohammad...

This *hadith* (a saying of the Prophet transmitted orally, not in the Qur'an) is often cited by Sufis.

ACKNOWLEDGEMENTS

To David Zieroth for the pleasure of great conversation, and for his discerning ear and insightful comments on earlier versions of the work— thank you. To Peter Midgley for opening the door and guiding the manuscript through the process; and to the expert and convivial team at The University of Alberta Press who transformed this ephemera into a three-dimensional reality—thank you. And to Alice Major for the editorial help, the gentle nudges, the punctuation sweep, the final shaping—and the tough questions—thank you.

I am especially indebted to my wife·Karen for her plain·speaking feedback, steadfast heart, and more than generous accompaniment on the lengthy journey.

The first three parts of "Nowhere in Sight" first appeared in *Prairie Fire*, Spring 2006.

"Water, Language, Faith" was first published as a chapbook by Alfred Gustav Press, 2008.

The first part of "Salt" first appeared in *CV2*, Summer 2013.

Portions of "Living on Air" first appeared in the June 2015 issue of *Literary Review of Canada*.

100 Days
Juliane Okot Bitek
978-1-77212-043-1 | $19.95 paper
978-1-77212-152-0 | $15.99 EPUB
978-1-77212-153-7 | $15.99 Kindle
978-1-77212-154-4 | $15.99 PDF
120 pages | Foreword, author's note
Robert Kroetsch Series
Poetry | Rwanda | Genocide

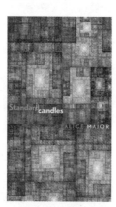

Standard candles
Alice Major
978-1-77212-091-2 | $19.95 paper
978-1-77212-116-2 | $15.99 EPUB
978-1-77212-117-9 | $15.99 Kindle
978-1-77212-118-6 | $15.99 PDF
176 pages | Notes
Robert Kroetsch Series
Poetry

Demeter Goes Skydiving
Susan McCaslin
978-0-88864-551-7 | $19.95 paper
978-0-88864-758-0 | $15.99 PDF
136 pages | Notes
A volume in cuRRents, a Canadian
literature series
Poetry | Canadian Literature
Women's Studies | International
Education | Development